MIRRAN THOUGHT

MIRRAN THOUGHT

Spitzwiesenstr. 50
90765 Fürth
Germany

www.dwmirran.de
www.empty.de
empty@empty.de

READ TWENTYONE
(MT-620)

Print and Publication by BOD
In de Tarpen 42
D-22848 Norderstedt
www.bod.de
info@bod.de

First printing 2019

MIRRAN THOUGHT is the publishing arm of
Mirran Threat, a company devoted to releasing the
music and writings of the various members of Doc
Wör Mirran. Mirran Thought and Mirran Threat are
both divisions of MT Undertainment.

THE GHOST OF EMPATHY

Western Haiku, Volume 10

Joseph B. Raimond

These pieces were written from 2014 to 2016 in Berlin, Paris, London, Munich, Darmstadt, Prague, Koblenz, Köln, Luxembourg, Rimini, San Marino, Cecina, Florence, Heidelberg, Manchester, Barcelona, Dublin and Adine.

As always, in loving memory of Frank Abendroth and Tom Murphy.

Dedicated to Oliver Sacks

For my beautiful Conny

Cover art "The Ghost Of Empathy" by Joseph B. Raimond, watercolor, acrylic and ink on paper, 2018.

This is DWM release Nr. 169

Berlin

Even the strength
Of the perpetual big city gray
Can't dim the light you give

The February buds
Might still be destined
For a frosty death

The miles that race past
Are stopped like from a magnet
By my longing for you

Big city dusk
Gray turns to black
Alcohol brings colour

Reminiscing, trading old stories
Like old war veterans
Backstage importance

Loud, louder, loudest
A contest of pain
The most ringing ears wins

Big hair, leather, chains
Who spent the most
To look the cheapest?

Tomorrow I will find
Your lips against mine
Anticipation

A record release party
For some band
No one will ever worship

On this stage
I got my fifteen minutes stardom
And free beer

The big city dog
Ignores the loud sirens
Of the passing police car

Here, in this city
Someone put up their walls
Here, we're taking ours down

Neither the fame nor the fortune
Can ever be had
From unreadable graffiti

Bloody tissue litter
The early morning bus-stop
Somewhere, someone is in pain

Quick body check, no pain
Nothing stolen. nothing missing
A sober morning ritual

The cryptic graffiti
Of an unknown artist
Will keep him unknown

Sober up, asshole
And put your dick away
You aint a teenage no mo'

Paris

Rusty nails and silence
Don't need to look
If a train is coming

Useless! Useless!
American fast food garbage
Littering the Parisian streets

Either endless fields, meadows
Or streets filled, grimy buildings
France is black or white

A cold beer in my hand
On the Eifel Tower, second level
Paid for with my soul

Useless! Useless!
Cowboy hats and chewing tobacco
Walking down a street in Paris

Six hundred seventy steps up
Six hundred seventy steps down
Cheapskates know the Eifel Tower

Useless! Useless!
A cripple on
The Eifel Tower steps

Clinging to the railing
Wild panic in her eyes
A woman with a fear of heights

The Eifel Tower sags
Under the weight
Of a thousand Japanese tourists

Don't know what is more inspiring
The panoramic view of the city
Or the pretty French girls

Punk-rock playing in my mind
Cars, trucks, traffic and sirens
Soundtrack of the city

An old newspaper
On a subway seat
I read yesterday's news

French bully, staring me down
He exits at the next stop
I feel relieved

Clanking and rocking
Wheels squealing, lurch to a stop
The efficient, ancient subway

Trucks, cars, trains
Even in the big city
The smell of spring

The fat American woman
Farted and
The whole Eifel Tower shook

The ghost of our broken love
Still haunts
The romantic streets of Paris

The sports car just drove by
A woman, warm wind in her hair
Must have been Lucy Jordan

Quick! Write down a haiku
While waiting in line
At the local fast food restaurant

Munich

Without compromise I stumble,
Lurch, from love to love
Never learning, never loving

Writing, painting…. Whatever
All a lame and futile attempt
For vanity to overcome eternity

Drunken, the football fans
Crowd the morning train into town
Singing their songs of glory

A brisk walk
In the Bavarian sun
And I almost feel young again

Legless, a big city beggar
Pulling his ass along the street
I give him my newspaper

White sausages, pretzel, a litre beer
Lederhosen, drunken song
Is this my adopted culture?

With its beer bellies, foul moods
Affluence, flatulence & arrogance
Munich doesn't inspire great art

London

Smelly tourists
Filling the airport bus
They will shower at home

Tame, grey squirrels
Begging for bits of chocolate
From overweight, sloppy tourists

The present, using up
More and more of the future
Shitting heaps of the past

While stepping off the plane
I can still
Taste your lips

The water begins to boil
For an instant coffee
A beggar can be choosey

In this land of tea
Give a coffee please
With clouds of rich milk

On the holiday journey
The child's thoughts
Are light years from school

Entering the clouds
The plane bumps and falls
Cold sweat on my forehead

Clackety clack
Thrown back and fourth
Trains were invented here

In the early morning hours
Party goers on their way home
Tourists pulling suitcases

Angry words and threats
As more people want on the bus
Than could ever fit

Although hours away yet
I can already feel
The warmth of your coming love

As the sun begins to set
A strange roommate
Will he snore?

A beautiful white swan
So very busy
Plucking feathers from her breast

Square miles of concrete
Not a speck of earth
Where does all the rain go?

Big city grime and rubbish
No nature, not a thing growing
But no wood ticks either

The doors close on my nose
The elevator goes up without me
The wait seems like eternity

The pint is slowly filled
Up to the rim, like it should be
Ice cold excellence

My loud sneeze
Startles my son
Showering in the bathroom

A small lap dog, sitting on a lap
Glares from the top, front window
Of a double decker bus

Your loving, open arms
Promise me a home
I will always return to

Such quality in our love
I won't fear death
With you at my side

Up on the third floor
Vibrations still give away
The passing of a tube train below

The plane didn't crash, so
I was destined
To live a bit longer

Where are the beans and potatoes
The sausage I was promised?
Where is the English breakfast?

Little children, sleepy
Uttering strange languages
In the hotel breakfast room

Oblivious to a coming tube train
A dirty grey mouse
Feasting on the tourist rubbish

Studying maps with camera ready
Dumpy clothes and stupid T-shirt
An international traveler

Darmstadt

Amid comments
Of gained weight
Mom's home cooking

Home is for reflecting
A gathering of fulfilled dreams
Perhaps a few regrets as well

Useless! Useless!
My mother
At a Star Trek convention

Love goes through the stomach
Not only for lovers
But also for family

Mom is getting old
So am I
And I seem to be catching up

Good, better, best
You have taught me
Superlatives

The tyrant is banished
Swearing, insults to a blank wall
And no one left to suffer

The trees might still be bare
But their buds
Promise me spring

Prague

The buzz of the birds and the bees
Is helped to blossom
By the buzz of a good beer

Walking through a beautiful city
He is playing the tourist
But is planning great art

A cup of coffee, then
A quick breakfast
Then out, to conquer the world

I can't imagine a more important
Invention, for the good of mankind
Than milk chocolate

Three lines, try to change your life
Now, only two lines left
Did I inspire you?

A strange café
Eating strange, foreign foods
The risks of travelling!

A day on the trains
A day of relaxing
A day of reflection

Holding the hand of my love
The reflection
Of a new city in her eyes

The strangeness of a foreign land
Can be expressed
In the strangeness of their toilets

As the keeper of the keys
Lock away my bad thoughts
Until dusty and dead

Don't let the clouds of age
Darken that gleam in your eyes
You will always be beautiful

Together we discover a city street
But as I take your hand
We discover what is in our hearts

With a beer in one hand
And whiskey in the other
I'm at home in any city

I don't let the big city guilt
Through the gates while
I'm after a good whiskey buzz

Köln

Football fans on a train
Discussions on the philosophy
Of the goalie's strategy

Illegible graffiti
Hide an author's message
At least it looks nice though

I stink of Kölsch
But that don't matter
I don't know anyone here anyway

A boy band singing in the sunshine
While I'm under a tree
Writing haiku poetry

Longing at a distance
Our bodies, so far apart
Anticipation strengthens our love

Don't even try to chat me up
I'm proudly, lovingly taken, by
Most beautiful girl in the world

Funny little summer insect
Lucky, you'll never know
The dreary drudgery of winter

Girls screaming for their boy band
No girls screaming for the poet
I did something majorly wrong

Broken big city people
Munching their fast food
Munching towards their death

No more Kölsch buzz
No more inspiration
No more haiku poems

Luxembourg

Passing the cemetery
I imagine all the slain, dead
Annoyed at the loud, passing train

A man cutting trees
The motor annoying me
As I drink my morning coffee

Nature's candy
Delights my tongue
Strawberries for breakfast

So far away
I miss the routine sounds
Of my lover in the morning

Time standing still
Little towns seem to sleep
A gentle fog over the river Mosel

A very important businessman
Typing on his notebook computer
Ignores the passing countryside

Fields of pretty flowers
I've no idea what they are called
Inspire nonetheless

The birds flying by
The lazy cows grazing
No animal would like to be human

Pulling a sweater
Over her eyes
My daughter tries to sleep

Lazy cows, munching their hay
Our train passing so close
The don't care, are used to it

Koblenz

An angry dog barking
But from the tenth floor
He looks so small and harmless

First the flash
Then the boom
Fireworks so far away

Daily commuters on the way home
Their daily routines
Will end someday

Overlooking a city
From a high-rise apartment
Would never get boring

A persistent wasp
Flew up to the tenth floor
Only to annoy me

An empty mailbox
Nothing can touch me
I am happy, today

I support the local economy
Everywhere I go
I drink lots of the local beer

A hundred waters was here
And I even knew him, a little
And that makes me relevant

Rimini

A California beach bum
White as cheese
Always at home on the Adria

The smell of the sea
Brings out the sailor in me
That I never was, nor want to be

A soft, fine brown sand
Though my fingers, my toes
In my eyes! In my hair!

From sea to shining sea
For me in my Italia
That aint so hard

A new town with a new love
Building on new experiences
Investing in what's left of a future

San Marino

That monstrous wave of guilt
Fading so fast, as I experience
A world without you

Even that little bit
Of my Italian blood
Lets me feel at home

In the torture museum
And I am left wondering
Why my ex-wife isn't on display

Cecina

Today, our middle sea
So quiet and tranquil
Like a pond, no waves

Even here, the ghost
Of a failed love
Haunts the peace of my travels

A little boy's sand castle
Invincible against the world's evil
No match for the tide

Put on my cool shades
So no one notices me
Staring at the bikini cleavage

Aha! But I saw you!
Crawling away sideways
A crab tries to hide

A blood thirsty sea monster?
No, just a piece of driftwood
A mother calming her son

Useless! Useless!
My 8 eye Dr. Martens street shoes
On the sandy Cecina beach

Florence

So much time to read
Lots of great coffee
A perfect holiday

An Italian taxi driver
Blocked by so many tourists
Today I learned new Italian words!

My cappuccino milk was round
But my girlfriend's was a heart
An Italian waiter hitting on my girl

An American tourist
With her mile wide, pink polyester
Bottom, taking pictures

Walking such timeless streets
It seems the door to death
Is now a bit further from my reach

While busy with the sightseeing
The tourist wasn't looking
Stepped into local dogshit

The tourists look up to the sights
The residents bored to the ground
I look strait at the cleavage

Street musicians play
Passers toss a guilty coin
Traditions of the loser's club

Forever going up
The escalator
Whether I'm on it or not

Adine

Roasting in the summer sun
With pretty green skin shining
A lizard scampers away

Useless! Useless!
An ice cold wind
Passes over these Tuscany hills

These poems are like porn
You are embarrassed to read
Hide from the wife

Real love is scratching
Each other's insect bites
In those hard to reach places

I support the local economy
Wherever I go I make sure
To drink lots of the local beer

I stop reading midsentence
Just to smell her hair
As she steps into a late morning

Grapes and olives
Line the endless
Rolling hills

Her hairdryer blowing
She's making herself beautiful
For our day together

Grandmother
A lifetime gone to dust
Would you have been proud?

Wisdom was achieved, finally
Not only through age
But also through excess

If only I was as immortal
As the eternal
Tuscany hills

So high
On the peak of a hill
A hawk soars below me

In September
The olive trees
Fear the coming winter

Waking up in Tuscany, where
The silence can be so complete
I hear music for the first time

Asleep in the Italian sunshine
The lazy cat
Has a life better than most people

Destiny at the wheel
Speeding, out of control
Crashing into the future

Do your lovers know
Of your sudden demise
Arms forever empty

That one last call
Your trembling voice
One last time in my ear

Your death, so final
Amplifies the fear in my eyes
Of my own final hours

My love for you was not hollow
Strength through bitterness
And weight by distance

Anger, frustration, love & loathing
How will I feel for you
Once the dust has settled?

Heidelberg

Forgiveness?
I haven't decided yet
But I don't need god to do it

The ego
To be fed, nurtured
Put up on a pedestal

Far away in that hospital
Someone else is lying in the bed
That my father just died in

We were born, we came
We conquered, were conquered
But we remain so meaningless

I was once a dumbass
Then I became scum
Now I've graduated to asshole

As a child I was here
Held a strange man's hand
Went crying to dad, who laughed

I see how other men stare
As you walk by
Still beautiful at fifty plus

Gardone Riviera

My lover's startled cry
A little water snake swims past
But a monster in her eyes

Dude, sorry about your little penis
How did I know?
The size of your car gave it away

Quick! Look! Danger danger!
I just saw the Garda great white
Why don't you believe me?

Although the waves are crashing
And the boat is rocking
Relief, as my stomach isn't turning

You and I. Here. Now.
Collecting shared memories
Together in life and love

As you fade forever to nothing
I, the pussy whipped European
Am here to save the world

As the least spiritual person
That was ever born
You should have been an atheist

You were never here, I think
Still, your unwanted ghost
Follows me wherever I go

So much like your father
Which is why
You are my sister no longer

If I let the horses free
Will they crash out of the gates
And never look back?

In our race towards death
You crossed the finish line first
Unfair! You started earlier!

Dee Dee died
That very moment
You turned your back on me

Manchester

Flying high in the sky
The clouds reflect the evening sun
Creating beauty beyond words

Funny sounding British accents
Help me conquer
My fear of flying

The jet engines roar
We zoom down the runway
The point of no return

The seemingly endless turbulences
Correspond to my adrenaline level
And my level of nervousness

How beautiful our world can be
My father will never again see
Makes for melancholy, this me

The rubbish lorry roared round
The custard coloured block of flats
Am I a bloody yankee wanker?

Dublin

All the forbidden flesh
Struttin' their stuff
Gobble while you can

I feel the lifeblood of this city
I don't feel your ghost
Let me stay here

Away from the tourists
To the worker's quarter pubs
I drink with the common man

I live near the dynamite factory
So be careful
What you say

Sunny afternoons, explore the city
Beer on the beach at night
The time to mourn you is over

Life is worth living
If only to bathe once
In the warm Mediterranean

While swimming, couldn't hold it
So I pissed in the vast sea
Think anyone noticed?

This is the last Haiku ever written
It was written by me
And read by nobody